Withered Roots

The Remnants of Eastern European Jewry

by
Stuart Farrell Tower

Illustrations by Barney Tower

Isaac Nathan Publishing Co., Inc.
Los Angeles
1994

To June
Very best wishes!
(and Thank you!)
Stuart F. Tower
11/98

Library of Congress Cataloging-in-Publication Data

Tower, Stuart Farrell
  Withered Roots:
      1. Judaica—Poetry   2. Eastern European History—Jewish
      3. Holocaust—Survivors, Interviews

ISBN: 0-914615-11-4   94-069189

10 9 8 7 6 5 4 3 2 1

Manufactured in the United States of America

Book and cover designed by Isaac Nathan Publishing Co., Inc.
Original Artwork © by Barney Tower

Published by the Isaac Nathan Publishing Co., Inc.
22711 Cass Avenue
Woodland Hills, (Los Angeles), CA 91364
Tel: (818) 225-9631
Fax: (818) 225-8354

INTRODUCTION

Today, the whole of Eastern Europe is changing political directions at a dizzying pace. New-found freedoms are spilling onto the streets of Warsaw, Cracow, Moscow, Kiev, St. Petersburg, Prague, Bratislava and Budapest ... and even to some degree in Sofia and Bucharest. Only in the former Yugoslavia have the guns of war gone far beyond the occasional skirmish of unrest.

Where does the isolated Jewish community stand in this fast-moving drama? Sadly, with instant freedom comes the instant antithesis, and the answer to that age-old question, "Is it good or bad for the Jews?" leans grimly toward the negative. Once officially suppressed, anti-Jewish sentiment is gaining notorious strength, and the finger of blame once again points menacingly at the well-worn scapegoat.

For the more than 125,000 Jews remaining in Eastern Europe, and the approximately 1,500,000 throughout the former Soviet Union, constant vigilance is the order of the day during these volatile times.

During the decade of the 1980's and into the 90's, I have travelled extensively throughout the region, seeking out, observing and interviewing the once highly-visible Jewish population. This has taken me from the Volga to the Oder, from the Danube to the Vistula - once the heart of the killing fields of the Holocaust. The most recent journey, surrounding the 50th anniversary of the Warsaw ghetto uprising, vividly pointed out the dramatic changes that have taken place since the series of earlier visits .

As in my book "Hear 0 Israel" (1983), I have elected to use a concise, yet descriptive structure which I refer to as "poetica Judaica", to help the reader sort out and digest the multifarious sights and sounds of Eastern Europe and the remnant within. Given the emotionally-charged content, my hope is that it will generate concern and compassion for this hardy minority who have stood alone for decades, no strangers to uncertain and perilous times.

Stuart Farrell Tower
Oxnard, California
1994

Singularly and lovingly dedicated
to the memory of....

Judith Tova Tower

who enthusiastically and warmly
welcomed the many adventures we
stumbled onto during our 40-year union -

"all that is sweet, multiplied
all that is beautiful, magnified
all that is good, personified"

CONTENTS

"once there were eleven million . . ."

The Former SOVIET UNION

EPILOGUE

ﻉﻩ

Poland

"Selektion" siding at Auschwitz II (Birkenau)

Can one travel to Eastern Europe and avoid any visual reference to the Shoah? Yes, of course. Can an ostrich bury it's head in the sand? It can, and often does. Oswiecim, once referred to as "Auschwitz" during the Nazi occupation, for example, serves as a magnetic reminder of the human species' inhumanity to the human species.

When traveling anywhere in this broad region of the European continent, all roads eventually lead to this most infamous of the death camps. For many, it takes two visits to each of the Auschwitz sites I and II (Birkenau)—to fully comprehend—seeing for the first time, and then years later again seeing, but most of all believing what had previously been seen and felt emotionally.

OSWIECIM

(Auschwitz)

approaching Oswiecim from the east
one is suddenly and rudely stunned
by the sight of giant smokestacks
spewing forth their brownish venom -
this is the way this living hell
has always been described
in thousands of tear-filled journals
and in the graphic words of Levi,
    Frankl and Wiesel,
emerging from the very shadows of
history's darkest hour

but...
nearly forty years have passed!

why are the crematoria
still belching
ashes of death into the sky?

a welcome reality comes to light
as the chemical plants of Oswiecim,
the main industry of this noted town,
    quickly emerge,
quieting this state of disbelief
(so this is what
    the chimneys represent ?)
an auspiciously bizarre beginning
to this sobering pilgrimage

busloads of tourists and school-children,
quiet, orderly and well-chaperoned,
from all over Poland, with some
    from neighboring lands,
pour into the bowels of infamy,
filing under the notorious wrought-iron
    entrance sign

into the chilly morning mist
well-clothed against the elements,
they tramp the mud-gravel streets,
alongside the once-electrified
barbed fences and stilted towers
in and out of the dreary brick barracks,
as did the millions in threadbare rags
when humankind crashed to its lowest ebb

walking on the birch-lined path
    from main camp to Birkenau,
the railroad platform so well-known
in countless versions and visions
where the final 'selektions' were made,
(you to the left - you to the right!)
sits in a pleasant meadow covered with
the stems of wild, yellow margaritkes,
    to bloom again come spring

and you think a wretched thought . . .
this scene borders on the blasphemous!
in this countryside of tranquility,
standing amid a bunch of damned daisies,
slender white trees and gawking children,
    burning questions seeking answers
        fill my groping mind
      in a desperate search for meaning

can a school child in Des Moines or Boston
Dallas Madrid Sydney Bombay
come to an understanding of this,
of what transpired here in these
killing fields of Poland?
can anyone who has not lived it,
who has not observed it,
this epitome of man's
inhumanity to man,
ever, ever even begin to realize
that the victims were not alone,
that all of civilization perished
each time a Zyklon-B can was opened
each time the blue crystals were dropped
each time the ovens were fired-up?

nearing the iron gate, about to leave,
the only words that seem to issue forth
from quivering throat and bone-dry lips,
begin with

"*Sh'ma Yisroel*"
as an affirmation of my faith
and end with an act of renewal and awe,

"magnified and sanctified
be
His Great Name...."

(I whisper *amen,* O let it be!)

I drift back into a void
of silence

&

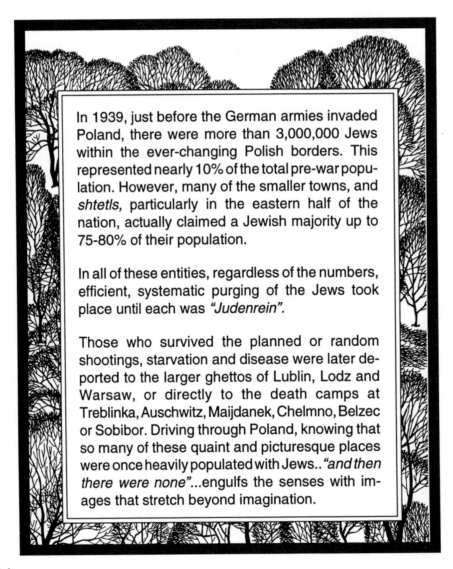

In 1939, just before the German armies invaded Poland, there were more than 3,000,000 Jews within the ever-changing Polish borders. This represented nearly 10% of the total pre-war population. However, many of the smaller towns, and *shtetls,* particularly in the eastern half of the nation, actually claimed a Jewish majority up to 75-80% of their population.

In all of these entities, regardless of the numbers, efficient, systematic purging of the Jews took place until each was *"Judenrein".*

Those who survived the planned or random shootings, starvation and disease were later deported to the larger ghettos of Lublin, Lodz and Warsaw, or directly to the death camps at Treblinka, Auschwitz, Maijdanek, Chelmno, Belzec or Sobibor. Driving through Poland, knowing that so many of these quaint and picturesque places were once heavily populated with Jews.. *"and then there were none"*...engulfs the senses with images that stretch beyond imagination.

SHTETL: 1983

I smell the smells
I hear the sounds
I visualize ... yet
the roads are not mud-covered,
     nor deep-rutted
they are smoothly paved and lined
the village scene once dominated
by the onion-dome upon the hill
now punctuated here and there by antennae
reaching from slated cottage roofs

this, then, is Poland, 1983 -
the railroad has ceased its nightly runs
the screams from cattle cars no longer heard
the rusted tracks overgrown with brush -
now the daffodils wilt in the frost of fall
while milch-cows roam the pasturelands
where tractors have replaced the plow

yes, the *shul* still stands, in ill-repair,
　　serving as the village hall
where petty-czars spout their party line
and the flag of state red, green and white
flies from the barren, faded arch
where once the Mogen Dovid proudly stood

the *shtetl* of 1983...
Judenrein ...Jew-free...
a mere whisper, echoing across the valley
　　of the shadow
　　　　　　of
　　　　　　　　death.

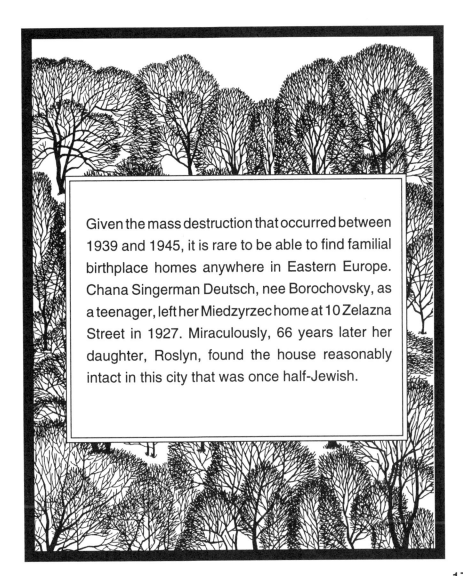

Given the mass destruction that occurred between 1939 and 1945, it is rare to be able to find familial birthplace homes anywhere in Eastern Europe. Chana Singerman Deutsch, nee Borochovsky, as a teenager, left her Miedzyrzec home at 10 Zelazna Street in 1927. Miraculously, 66 years later her daughter, Roslyn, found the house reasonably intact in this city that was once half-Jewish.

ZELAZNA 10

vu iz dus gesele?
vu iz die shtieb?
(gdye eta ulitsa, gdye eta dom?)
where is the street, where is the house?
(from an old Jewish/Russian folk song)

The street
    the house
        the town
           still stand
once in the battle-path
of ten thousand steel treads,
fire-spewing riveted dragons,
white swastikas thundering eastward,
red stars retaliating to the west -

this is Miedzyrzec Podlaski !

withstanding the ravaging storm,
the tensions of tenuous calm,
uncertainties of a new regime -

now ethnically cleansed,
    devoid of Abraham's flock-
now squatting at the crossroads
    of emptiness -

O Chana, daughter of old Poland,
you have sent your own blood
deep into a *world* gone by,
turning back the pages of time

to rediscover Zelazna 10

entranced, she somberly walks
where you in your youth once
    strolled -

now, questioning the inanimate,

"What have you seen through your
windows, Zelazna 10?
you have kept so many warm from
      the cold,
    dry from the rains -
you are panes and chimney
you are walls and frame
    doorways and halls
    shutters and roof -
you have stoutly weathered
    the years -
you will outlive us all,
    Zelazna 10 ...

do vidzhenia! forever, farewell"

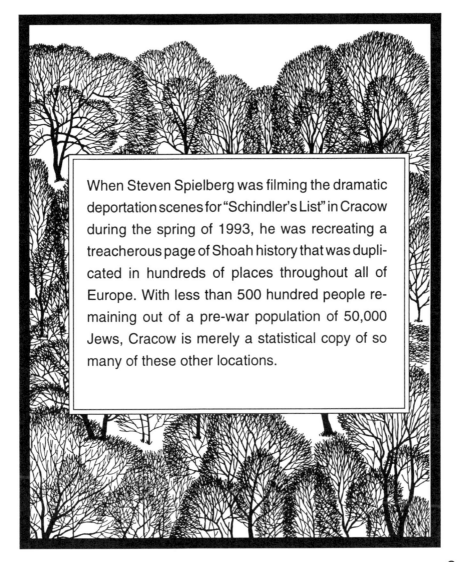

When Steven Spielberg was filming the dramatic deportation scenes for "Schindler's List" in Cracow during the spring of 1993, he was recreating a treacherous page of Shoah history that was duplicated in hundreds of places throughout all of Europe. With less than 500 hundred people remaining out of a pre-war population of 50,000 Jews, Cracow is merely a statistical copy of so many of these other locations.

THE LAST JEWS OF CRACOW

winding through the Tatras,
rugged Carpathian slopes
into snow-dusted Zakopane -
the road to Cracow
levels off in lengthy
curveless stretches
the city soon appears
along the Vistula -
at its entrance, Wawel Hill,
with castle and cathedral,
reminders of era's past
when Cracow reigned supreme
as Poland's capital -
the sweet trumpet blares
the never-finished tune
from St. Mary's tower,
on Main Market Square

amid this medieval splendor,
a flash-back could occur
to yet another time,
when Hans Frank quartered here
as Governor of Occupied Poland -
this very essence of arrogance,
President of the Academy
of German Law, no less,
vowed to reduce the Jews
from a dangerous three-million
"and then there were none . . ."

as for Cracow's very own,
a *Judenrein* state was
painfully achieved in
    early 1943,
when the last of the ghetto
were liquidated by mass
deportations to Treblinka,
code-named "T-2" by Frank,
forever the pompous lawyer,
(a most redundant phrase)

Reb Mendele Lebovicz
a frail whisper of a man,
sitting on a broken bench
in the antiquated Remu shul,
defies these woeful numbers -
sent to labor camps deep
within the Reichland, he had
the youthful strength
and luck to survive -
Reb Mendele and a few hundred
now make their final stand here,
still avoiding Skawinska Street
and the old Kazimierz quarter,
sanctified by 50,000 souls -

these are truly and sadly
the last Jews of Cracow

(Herr Frank tried suicide before he died
in the hangman's noose at Nuremberg)

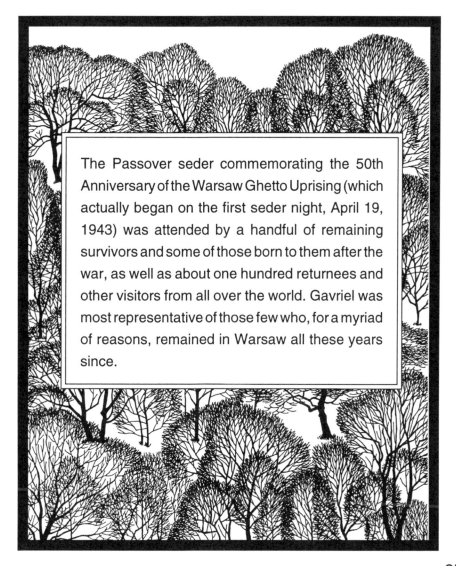

The Passover seder commemorating the 50th Anniversary of the Warsaw Ghetto Uprising (which actually began on the first seder night, April 19, 1943) was attended by a handful of remaining survivors and some of those born to them after the war, as well as about one hundred returnees and other visitors from all over the world. Gavriel was most representative of those few who, for a myriad of reasons, remained in Warsaw all these years since.

GAVRIEL

I

Why Is This Night Different?

across the lengthy table
in the crowded seder hall
he sits -
    hunched over a steaming
      bowl of soup -
this child of the darkest night
in a millennia of dark nights,
his broken teeth gray with decay,
the shaggiest of straggly beards
red-stained with the fruit of the
      vine -
will the gauntness ever leave his eyes?

he looks down at the fatty liquid
    and spoons the last drop
with an urgency only few can fathom

II

Traces

the ghetto,
once melted down to dust,
now,
sanctified by granite slabs -
now,
left with scant few traces
of an era all but forgotten
by a world of terminal apathy

on this spot stood the prison,
and there the bunkers lay-
and here the Umschlagplatz,
the final deportation station
where soldiers of the Pharoah
herded in the Hebrew slaves
when the sea could not be parted -
(there would be no exodus here)

now,
the ranks of Polish unemployed
drink ale at the tavern on Mila

III

Am Yisroel Chai
(The Children of Israel Live!)

Gavriel ben Avrum,
messenger of his God,
speaks:

  "I smuggled
   weapons and food
   from the other side . . .

   I remained
   when night became dawn . . .

   I have outlasted
   the furies of hell . . .

   Yes , yes !
   the children's cries were heard -
   for I am witness to it all . . ."

and these haunting words
from this troubled child
in his seventh decade
hold a meaning beyond reason . . .

In Shoah terms, Eastern Europe is referred to as a massive killing-field, a cemetery, and symbolically, a forest of stone. Hence, *"The Stone Forest Trilogy"*.

THE STONE FOREST TRILOGY

I. PRAGUE
(on visiting the ancient cemetery in
Prague's Jewish Town)

seeking out this walled-in corner,
a maze-like forest
      of eroding stone,
this resting place from medieval time
forms an endless montage of *alef, bet* -
a layered landscape of tilting steles
      recounting countless tribulations

a mass of *"kvittlech,"* notes to heaven,
nestling at Rabbi Loew's grave,
his "golem" standing endless guard -

Praha, city fair, you have honored
history well, preserving this *precious legacy*
      of hallowed ground

II. ZHIDOVSKI CMENTARZH
(Miedzyrzec Podlaski, Eastern Poland)

zhidovski cmentarzh - resting place of the Jew
    empty, composted field of dry bones -
a near-stoneless forest, pillaged by the vandals
      of time,
overtaken by the mossy growth of fifty years -

in a solitary stance, a monument to unspeakable
      times
      cries to be seen,
its granite smoothness begging to be touched
    by the living -

"We hear you - we heed the voices of
      martyrdom -

    you are not to be forgotten
    we embrace you
    we are here - we are here!"

in parting, climbing over the crumbling wall,
we pause . . . to reaffirm the ancient faith for
those departed minyans of Miedzyrzec

    "yisgadal, vyiskadash -
    magnified and sanctified, is the holy. . ."
              amen

III. TREBLINKA
(a name that lives in perpetual infamy)

the sun has set beyond the pines,
we are only two amid the mass
of chiseled stone in rolling fields
atop the consecrated ash
as stillness permeates the dusk -
a rail-stop in the countryside
appearing so pastoral and serene
where box-cars of human cargo
from Warsaw and Bialystok
fueled the furnaces of finality
stoked by mercenary hordes

boldly inscribed,
"never again" screams forth
from the monument upon the hill -

while two days travel to the south

Bosnia burns

(Editor's Choice Award, National Library of Poetry, 1994)

Czech Republic and Slovakia

The long-abandoned synagogue at Ruzemberok, Slovakia

The mental picture of trains and their sealed freight cars transporting men, women and children to their eventual deaths by gas, starvation, bullets or disease, is perhaps the most enduring and vivid of all Shoah imagery. So much so, that Washington's U.S. Holocaust Museum's remarkable and powerful presentations include an exact replica of one of the freight wagons of the era.

TRAINS

Kosice is a rail-head
a junction where tracks divide
to the north, south, east, west
and all directions in between -
rolling-stock of every kind
steaming through each day
and far into the night -
a veritable rail-buffs dream

this Ruthenian trading post of
quaint half-timbered homes
is a European provincial
picture post-card perfect town
in any travel agent's file -

yet those of the remnant few
shudder at the sound of its name -
for here one's life or death was chosen
by systematic callous dregs who
scheduled the transport destination

Treblinka, Belzec to the north,
Oswiecim (Auschwitz) due northwest,
Maidenek, Sobibor and points northeast -

west, only west held out some hope,
for factory work inside the Reich
prolonged life for those
who were young or strong enough

Kosice, or Kassa *(in Hungarian)* -
railroad, trains and tracks,
wagons and engines and tenders,
signals and screeching brakes,
the oily smell of hell on earth
and the thump-thump, clickety-clack,
rattling sounds of metal-to-metal

those who remember all-too-well
whenever they see or hear a train,
        recall the Kassa of yesterday,
re-stoking their furnace of fear
                to this day,
            and from this day on,
        for generations yet to come

The forceably abandoned houses of worship located throughout the region can be found in every town where at least a few *minyans* of Jews resided at one time. The local populace can never be accused of lacking creativity, having restored these sometimes simple, sometimes ornate synagogues into everything from meeting halls to grain storage houses, from town offices to movie theaters (including a porno theater in Kazmierz Dolny). In some rare cases, the rotting buildings still stand - unused, unheralded, unmarked. Ruth Gruber's book, *"Jewish Heritage Travel"* is the most complete guide to cemeteries and synagogues, their current status and exact locations.

YIZKOR 1993

(on the discovery of an abandoned synagogue -
Ruzemberok, Slovakia)

appearing as a derelict ship
beached upon this mud-rutted path,
a graying-white, red-trimmed relic,
a fading spectre of another time -

on entering this ghostly apparition
steel-sculpted unhinged doors
      give way
to a cavernous sea of broken glass

speechless, frozen in mid-thought,
suspended in a vacuum of a half-century,
the mind fills with vivid imagery

of

doors, once again upright
stained-glass shards in place
polished pews around the bimah
papas and sons in a somber mood
womenfolk in the gallery above
Rabbi, wrapped in fringed garment
        facing to the east,
the portly chazzan begins the Yizkor
        chant
    in a muted liturgy -

for
there is no sound to be heard
in this surrealistic pantomime

as
these mere figments of ash
will soon waft away . . .

as quickly as this scene arrives
it vanishes -
the rancid aroma of decay returns
borne by the bony arms
of civilization's lowest form

Hungary

Imre Varga's "Weeping Willow" Holocaust Memorial-Great Synagogue, Budapest

Archival Drawing

Raoul Wallenberg, whose legendary role in personally saving tens of thousands of Hungarian Jews from deportation and certain death, remains at the head of the distinguished group of righteous Gentiles who risked their very lives so that others could survive the war against the Jews. His name is greatly honored by peace-loving human beings everywhere, but nowhere with such reverence as in today's Budapest.

BLUE FLAGS OVER BUDAPEST

walking toward Dohany Street,
dragging on a stubby cigarette,
   he wildly gestures

"here, there, and over there -
these were some of the 'safe houses'
blue flags with yellow crosses
protected those within . . ."

he points to the Great Synagogue,
   a behemoth of a building,
noting that it was the 'holding pen'
where the 'selekt' ate molding bread
while waiting days and even weeks
for their deportation to oblivion

Gyula Drechsler's voice trails off,
he crosses the street in a half-trot,
   we skip along to keep pace,
but his short legs on a five-four frame
are like pistons, bless him!

now he goes on in a rich mixture of
Yiddish, peppered with fractured English,
emitting a raging stream-of-consciousness

"near the end of '44 we lived in that greystone
building on the corner as part of a hastily-
fashioned ghetto 60,000 down-trodden crowded
into less than two-hundred such places can you
believe that my Sari and I you will meet her soon
were married a few months before everyone
thought we were insane for marrying at such a
time we were all somewhat mad anyway we
escaped the ghetto with a group of *Chalutzim* and
false papers crossed the Danube to the Buda side
many of our young friends did the same
Eichman's *'Kommando'* yes the very same was
quartered in the city he called us *'vilde junge
Juden'* as well he might have but in our miserable
condition we were nearly harmless we had more
fear for the Arrow Cross than for the Deutsche
those bastard Magyars hated Jews with a passion
second to none even the Hun they wantonly
murdered with a lust beyond human
understanding but we were starving our only
thought after a while was food for three months
we raided the farmlands in the countryside
ranging south to the shores of Lake Balaton
foraging by night and hiding by day until we
finally met up with advance Red Army patrols
and learned that the battle for Budapest was
over . . ."

he pauses to light another cigarette
and we welcome the chance to rest -

deeply inhaling, he goes on slowly

    "we learned that all four of our parents
    perished on the forced march to Austria
    days before the beginning of the end . . .

    (pause)

    though Wallenberg saved many
    thousands
    a real *'messiah'* that Swede -
    his blue flags flew so defiantly
    as if this were Stockholm!

    may he be in peace
    wherever he may be......

we chorus an *"omayn"* to that thought
for the most righteous of the righteous

at the door to his apartment he relaxes,
smiles

"come, my friends, we will have some tea
and we will talk . . . we will talk . . ."

and he talked

and we listened

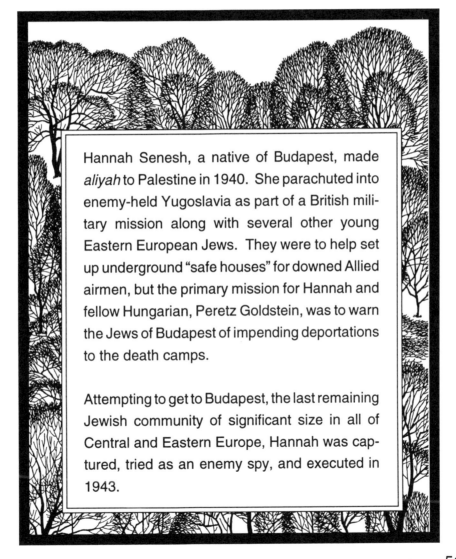

Hannah Senesh, a native of Budapest, made *aliyah* to Palestine in 1940. She parachuted into enemy-held Yugoslavia as part of a British military mission along with several other young Eastern European Jews. They were to help set up underground "safe houses" for downed Allied airmen, but the primary mission for Hannah and fellow Hungarian, Peretz Goldstein, was to warn the Jews of Budapest of impending deportations to the death camps.

Attempting to get to Budapest, the last remaining Jewish community of significant size in all of Central and Eastern Europe, Hannah was captured, tried as an enemy spy, and executed in 1943.

HANNAH

in the Margit Prison courtyard
a slight child-Jewess stands
shivering in November's cold
dressed in a cotton skirt

just that morning she defiantly
lashed out at her Inquisitor
asking for no mercy from such as he

there is a stillness in the air
the flurries begin to thicken
the order is crisply shouted
the shots ring out to be heard all over
           Budapest

a spreading crimson circle
darkens the pure white silk
as droplets touch the virgin snow
amid the hollow, haunting echoes

"blessed is the match"
that kindles the eternal flame
for the sacred legend of
Hannah

the former Yugoslavia

The ancient arched bridge at Mostar—recently damaged by heavy shelling

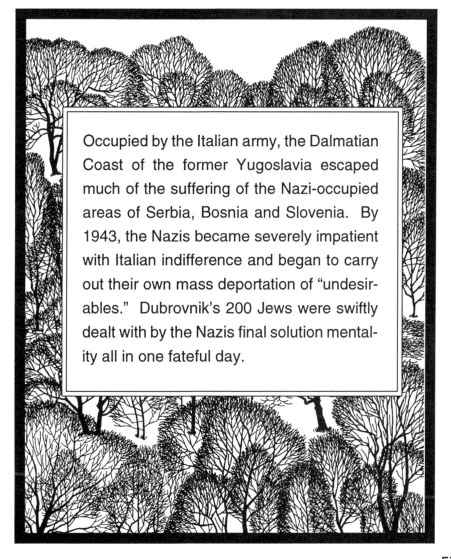

Occupied by the Italian army, the Dalmatian Coast of the former Yugoslavia escaped much of the suffering of the Nazi-occupied areas of Serbia, Bosnia and Slovenia. By 1943, the Nazis became severely impatient with Italian indifference and began to carry out their own mass deportation of "undesir-ables." Dubrovnik's 200 Jews were swiftly dealt with by the Nazis final solution mentality all in one fateful day.

THE SPRING OF '43

that April day has rarely been recalled-
    two hundred marching souls, two-by-two,
    four hundred heels clicking in cadence
    down steep and narrow cobbled lanes,
        under guard,
      across the sun-kissed *placa*
        to the city pier

"Shnell! Shnell! Place your luggage
on the steps - it will be sent along!"

and here, an ironic "gesture macabre" . . .
life preservers are issued to the lifeless -
a single and ancient vessel waits at dockside -
in a tenth of this final hour they clamber aboard
in knowing silence -
with the stench of rotting fish
filling the salty air
they slowly sail off on this splintered ark,
unlike Noah and his flock,
never again to be seen . . .

today's sun shines brightly, bouncing off each
red-tiled roof,
baking alabaster touring Teutons basking in its rays,
the *placa's* smooth slabs smothered
by northern hordes -

this is Dubrovnik/Ragusa,
Queen City of the Adriatic,
where no one seems to remember that day in spring,
   that non-existent day of the disappearing Jew -

there will be no recitation of the Kaddish here,
   for this speck-fraction of six million,

    now,

     or ever

Rivka Schlossberg (nee Pardo) is secretary and official greeter at the old Sephardic *sinagoga* in Sarajevo. Her great-grandfather was the Chief Rabbi during the period of Turkish rule. Rivka was one of 1,000 to survive the infamous Jasenovac concentration camp, but her husband and 11,000 other Sarajevo Jews died in the various death camps of Europe.

MARTYROLOGY SLAV

Yugoslavian highlands - the craggy karst
limestone-white on emerald-green,
under early autumn's frost

the mosques of Sarajevo recalling Ottoman rule,
Mostar's graceful ancient bridge, arching over the
stream,

while Tito's Travnik nestles in the pines,
basking in the glory of its heroic past
when partisans roamed the valleys and the hills

majestic Dubrovnik stands on the Adriatic shore,
yellowing tones against the azure sea

these were the sights of martyrdom, many years ago,
on another October morn in maddening times

the dark-eyed Rivka, descendent of Grand Rabbis,
       Sephardic daughter of the realm
speaks softly, slowly, of near-forgotten deeds -
the survivor of the infamous Jasenovac camp
sheds a flow of tears for those who perished,
painfully reciting each of the martyr's names . . .

"Rabbi of Dubrovnik, Solomon Baruch
Rabbi of Mostar, David Perrera
Rabbi of Travnik, Yitzhok Baruch
Rabbi of Split, Yitzchok Finzi
Rabbi of Donja Michalojac, Natan Schwartz
Chazzan of Djakova, Alexander Roth

each had refused to preach compliance
each had defied orders of the beast
each was slain on the same dark day
with the whisper of *"shema"* on his
                quivering lips . . .
thus, in that godless world was God affirmed!"

now Sarajevo displays a festive air,
awaiting its heralded winter games,
and Rivka's shul is on a renovation list
(with the city council's self-serving assist)

as she still weeps for the Slavic Jew -

Sarajevo
1983

Bulgaria

Old boats sailed silently southward in the night, their frightened passengers fleeing the nazi storm.

—Archival photo

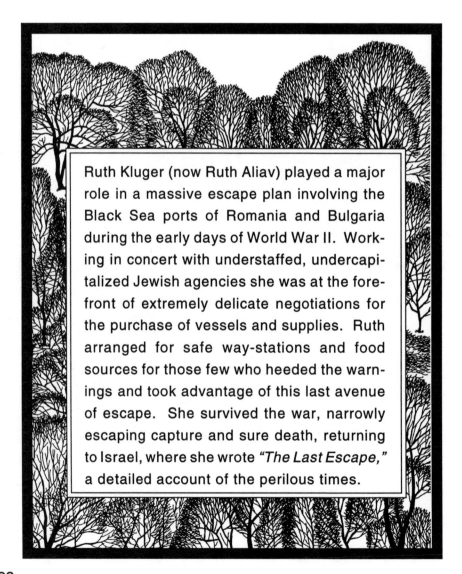

Ruth Kluger (now Ruth Aliav) played a major role in a massive escape plan involving the Black Sea ports of Romania and Bulgaria during the early days of World War II. Working in concert with understaffed, undercapitalized Jewish agencies she was at the forefront of extremely delicate negotiations for the purchase of vessels and supplies. Ruth arranged for safe way-stations and food sources for those few who heeded the warnings and took advantage of this last avenue of escape. She survived the war, narrowly escaping capture and sure death, returning to Israel, where she wrote *"The Last Escape,"* a detailed account of the perilous times.

RUTH

Running on hard-packed sand at water's edge
I stop to rest and gaze at the calm Black Sea,
knowing well that it had swallowed boat-loads
of the human flotsam in their attempts to flee

Romanian Constantza and Bulgarian Balchik,
and Varna to the south, meant freedom to
the fortunate few who had come this far,
waiting for their voyage to *Gan Eden*

long before unbelieving powers raised their hand
these ports of last resort had played a part
in the courageous schemes of one named Ruth,
the daring young Jewess of deeds yet unsung

fraught with dangers of the perilous times
with even derelict vessels difficult to find,
and alternative routes appearing more grim,
    these noble rescue efforts fell far short

the "Salvador" and the "Struma", memorialized,
    infamous sagas with a tragic loss of life,
though there were other unseaworthy hulks
    that sailed through to illegal safe havens

plodding back along the lonely silver strand,
    I could not help confront a dreadful truth -
how many more could have reached the Holy Land
had we, the sheltered, stood beside

    heroic Ruth

the Black Sea coast,
Varna, Bulgaria

Romania

Moshe Rosen (1911-1994), Chief Rabbi of Romania

Sighet - Elie Wiesel was born here in 1928. In the spring of 1944 the entire Jewish population was caught in the Nazi deportation web. Elie survived a series of death camps while losing his immediate family. He has since become the most eloquent, widely-read messenger of the Holocaust. In 1986, Elie Wiesel received the universally-prestigious Nobel Peace Prize.

THE CONSCIENCE
(Hamatzpun)

Eliezer
> my conscience

Eliezer
> your conscience

boyhood conscience of Romania-past
> lucid conscience of a mania-past

you must never
> be stilled by the blank stare of apathy

you must forever
> bear the thread-bare mantle of morality

for man
> who has so long been amoral

you have led us through the darkest night
and shared with us the promise of dawn,
onward, through the gates of the forest
    to the town beyond the wall -
and when memories again began to fade
    you gave a voice to Jews of silence -
the more faithful your memory,
    the more painful our reality

ah, Eliezer, your *Hasidishe zeydeh,*
who stoked the flames within your being,
whispers to you from beyond the storm

    Eliezer
        a soul on fire

though you speak
 as a living messenger of the dead
though you weep
    from the pangs of an anguished heart
though you write
    with ink of indelible blood

        your word remains unheard
        and if heard . . . unheeded

        Eliezer
            my conscience
        Eliezer
            your conscience
        Eliezer
            our brother

        conscience for a world
        that has no other

        Eliezer
                    hamatzpun

SIGHET
(Sighet, Maramures, Transylvanian Region of Romania)

This was Elie's place of birth, 1928 . . .

                    but
where are your Jews, today, Sighet?
fifteen-thousand souls - do you remember?
fragile puppets, dangling on strings,
dancing off through the theater wings
                    for one final exit . . .

where are your Jews, Sighet?

where are your synagogues
        and the chanting that echoed from within?
where are those strains of animated Yiddish,
        sing-song bargaining at the market-place?
can you ever recapture the flavor, Sighet?

haunted by reality, taunted by despair,
asking, probing, searching everywhere
for even a trace of the nail-holes
where the Shema had once been held
to the doorposts of Sighet,
well-covered now, by the paint of forty years . . .

where are your Jews, Sighet?

we wept for them, Sighet,
as we did for those in Lodz and Vilna,
        in Warsaw and Prague,
and for a thousand pin-points on the face
        of Europe,
    from the Urals to the Alps
    from the Baltic to the Balkans . . .

where are your Jews, Sighet?

the world must never forget,
for your native son shakes its conscience . . .
he causes us to quiver at the mention of you,
                    Sighet,
just as we quake in memory of Babi-Yar

you, too, Sighet, are Bialik's City of Slaughter,
one more name in the long, dark line of Kishinevs. . .

where are your Jews,
                    today,
                              Sighet?

YOSSI NACHMAN'S RETURN

Standing in the courtyard of the Brasov shul,
autumn's chill engulfing every Yiddish word . . .

"I am Yossi Nachman - born here in Brasov -
as was my father, of blessed memory, and
       his father before him -
of course I returned - what else could I do?
       (I had no answer . . .)
when the Red Army rescued us from Pechora,
I had already lost everything - and everyone -
       everyone - do you understand?
       (I had no answer . . .)

six-thousand deported to starvation on the Dniester
one hundred straggled back to our beloved Brasov -
a game of numbers, *Amerikaneh,*
     and no one ever wins!"

inside the shul, colder yet, the lights are dim
while two more await another eight, in vain -
Yossi, the third, and I, the fourth - not enough -
(my wife can never count among these minyan-poor)

along the lampless, winding downhill street
we walk in silence, wrapped in private thought,
knowing full-well that we shall never again meet
we say our *"zei gesunts,"* embracing Yossi Nachman

who soon fades into the dark of night

the Transylvanian Alps surround the ancient town
as sunrise shows the early snow
      upon Poiana's peaks
I awake to see a vision of that cobbled courtyard
and once again the returning remnant speaks . . .

"So how do you like *mein sheineh* mountains?
    (pause)
Do you now see why I came back to Brasov?
    (pause)

Nu, maybe next year in *Yerushalayim* . . . ?"

(I had no answers . . .)

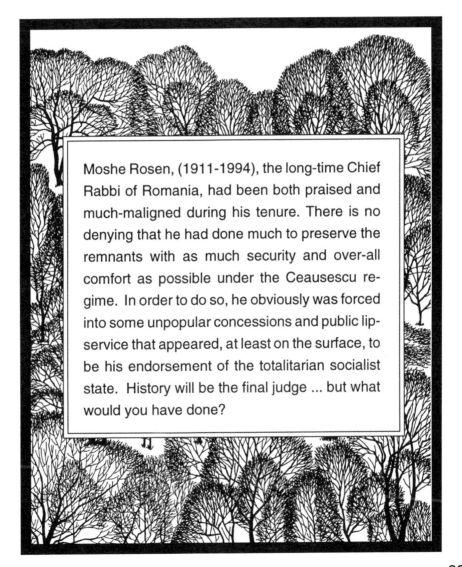

Moshe Rosen, (1911-1994), the long-time Chief Rabbi of Romania, had been both praised and much-maligned during his tenure. There is no denying that he had done much to preserve the remnants with as much security and over-all comfort as possible under the Ceausescu regime. In order to do so, he obviously was forced into some unpopular concessions and public lip-service that appeared, at least on the surface, to be his endorsement of the totalitarian socialist state. History will be the final judge ... but what would you have done?

THREE JEWS OF BUCHAREST
(Drei Yidden fun Bucureshti)

I.

Behold, His Eminence, The Chief Rabbi

    elegantly garbed in flowing purple robe,
    golden chain of office heavy on his breast -
    appearing pompous, yet of gentle bearing,

        he speaks:

    "I, Rebbe Moisheh, know my flock so well,
        my thirty-thousand -
    no, they do not despair any longer -
    contented for the most part, yes!
    for they know that their Rebbe keeps
    a wary eye for their welfare

    am I not Chief Rebbe for three decades now?
    do I not sit with the Grand National Assembly?
    have I not been decorated with the Star of the
        Republic?

alas, though I walk in the footsteps of my
dear, late father, the Gaon, Avram Leib,
scholar and Rebbe of Moineshti, Falticeni,
    and   Bucureshti,
I cannot   erase their holocaustic nightmares
    of the massacre at Iasi
    of starvation in Bucovina
    of Transniestria transports

but I have won a semblance of *Yiddishkeit*

    with
    kosher   kitchens
    and ritual baths,
    matzoth for Pesach
    and homes for the aging,
    Talmud Torah schools
    throughout the land -

I, Rebbe Moisheh,can proudly proclaim
that no Jew goes homeless or hungry . . .
.. . . and every child is taught the Words!"

he pauses with eyes closed,
as if in a trance,
rocks to and fro, as softly
he chants:

"Verily, I, Rebbe Moisheh, will lead my remnants
into God's Kingdom,
as Moisheh Rabbenu led the Children of Israel
out of the wilderness

. . . *omayn!*"

THREE JEWS OF BUCHAREST
(continued)

II.

Now, behold, the *Mashgiach,*

    Reb Fleisher, a most fitting name,
    Grand Master of the stewing-pot,
    in smock of grease-stained white,
    shaggy beard of lemon-orange flame -

    "*nu, nu,* come into my dining hall,
    it is my privilege to host you -
        but, please,
    in advance, seven dollars American,
        yes?

    no, no, you must not sit with my patrons,
        '*tor nisht!*'
      no, do not ask why -
    here! this table in the corner is for you

hah! you are trying to make eye-contact
with them?
you see, they do not glance back!
they,
even the young students by the window,
will not return your stares!

oy, my dear, naive *Amerikaneh,* now
you surely understand,
. . . they are all simply . . . cautious!
yes, yes, I know what His Eminence
told you -
perhaps true, but they do not know,
therefore they do not trust -
how do any of us know just
who you are...eh?

for us, the mere remnant, a stranger
breeds fear -
now you know why I seat you alone!

ess, ess, Amerikaneh, enjoy your meal -
the finest *'mamaliga'* in all of
Romania ... !"

THREE JEWS OF BUCHAREST
(continued)

III.

Lastly, behold, the third Jew of Bucharest,

Iancu Livadaru, the Curator,
resplendent in jaunty black beret
he leads the way
into the darkened vestibule
of the old Vacareshti tailor's shul

and beyond

into it's chamber of the unspeakable,
a museum of the Jew in Romania -
blood-caked history, under glass -
centuries of pillaging and pogroms,
deportations and death squads -
cossacks from the east
Einsatzgruppen from the west,
and always
the insidious Iron Guard from within . . .

the Curator stops in the midst of an
impassioned delivery:

"Amerikaneh, they **are** still afraid!
we **all** are - memories can never fade -
look around and you will see!
for we who make our final stand in the
Socialist Republic of Romania,
for us, the scattered few,

fear
has been a lifetime bedfellow

our heritage
from generations past,
our legacy
to the remnant,
from these remnants . . ."

he makes a sweeping gesture,
tries in vain to hide his tears -

"fuhrt gesunt, mein Amerikaneh,
go in health!"

the former
Soviet Union

Jewish woman and child, Bukhara, Uzbekistan

MOSKVA NIGHTS

(Succoth Eve: 1985)

Arkhipova Street, under dim light tonight,
its old lamps emitting an eerie glow -
militia ringing the old synagogue
as fifty congregants begin to file
down the steps, in orderly style

The Feast of Tabernacles has begun -
   Come, let us all rejoice!

"*Paidyom Paidyom! Priyamo!* Move along!
Do not stop . . . leave the area!"

Just to greet anyone is our simple goal-
not one fellow Jew seems open to talk,
as they now burst into a faster walk

This is Moscow in pre-*glasnost* times
The Union of Soviet Socialist Republics,
the State Almighty , without God, over all

Around the corner, out of "Ivan's" sight,
one woman stops to speak in Yiddish . . .
"I have a sister in Philadelphia. Please
       telephone her"
a number is passed as her bus arrives -
in a moment she is gone

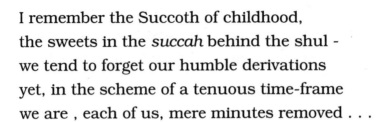

I remember the Succoth of childhood,
the sweets in the *succah* behind the shul -
we tend to forget our humble derivations
yet, in the scheme of a tenuous time-frame
we are , each of us, mere minutes removed . . .

(there, but for the grace of God . . . !)

The Feast of Tabernacles has begun -
Come, let us all rejoice!

David and Mila - The Shrayers finally were allowed to exit, along with their son Maxim, and after a few years in Israel, emigrated to Providence, Rhode Island. Maxim received his Ph.D from Yale University in 1993.

DAVID AND MILA

He, the doctor, can no longer practice
She, the teacher, must never again teach

their careers ended the day they applied
for exit permission

this is the all-too-familiar tragedy of
David and Mila Shrayer

the Moscow flat is cheerfully bright
an exception to the Soviet rule
as are both of this courageous pair
despite their non-person status

once a teacher of English, Mila relates
the new dilemma adding to their pain -
that should they finally be allowed to leave
the seven-year wait shall have been in vain -

"our son has been admitted
to a university of choice -
now he would be omitted
    from our visa -
we shall never go without him -
our quest is all for nought!"

the tea is poured in silence . . .
what can one say to this quandary?

another puzzle
    from this enigmatic land

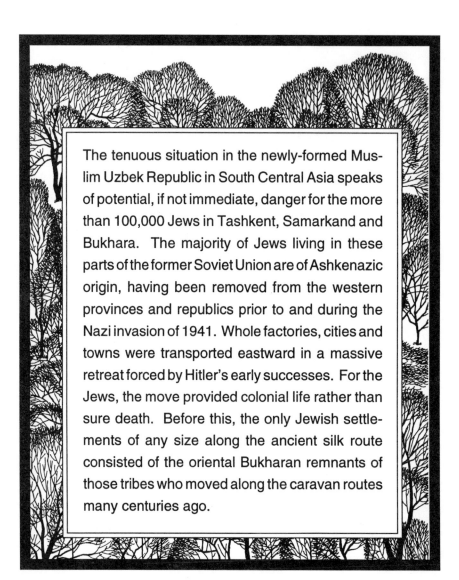

The tenuous situation in the newly-formed Muslim Uzbek Republic in South Central Asia speaks of potential, if not immediate, danger for the more than 100,000 Jews in Tashkent, Samarkand and Bukhara. The majority of Jews living in these parts of the former Soviet Union are of Ashkenazic origin, having been removed from the western provinces and republics prior to and during the Nazi invasion of 1941. Whole factories, cities and towns were transported eastward in a massive retreat forced by Hitler's early successes. For the Jews, the move provided colonial life rather than sure death. Before this, the only Jewish settlements of any size along the ancient silk route consisted of the oriental Bukharan remnants of those tribes who moved along the caravan routes many centuries ago.

TORAH IN TASHKENT

Moscow to Tashkent - light-years apart -
mosques and palms replace the Kremlin walls,
where silk-route eastern cultures meet the west -
Tashkent - overgrown oasis under Asian skies,
from caravansary to cosmopolis in a wink

Simchat Torah! let us celebrate the given Word!

In Moskva, that somber scene of Succoth
gives way to sheer abandon on the street
with dancing and embracing multitudes

while here in remote Uzbekistan
where Ashkenazim and the Bukharan
maintain distinctly separate ways
it's just the scattered few tonight
     in the Ashkenazic mini-shul

although subdued, a warmth comes shining through
(a vaguely-explained phenomenon, wherever
Jew meets Jew!)
the slivovitz and the vodka freely flow
as the toasting centers on the four of us

"Lang leben Ahmyeereekee!
Lang leben unsereh Yidden!
Lang leben unsereh
Ahmyeereekahnskeeyeh
lantzleiter!"

Simchat Torah! let us dance with the Holy Scrolls!

'round and 'round the bimah
in Tashkent!

WOMAN OF BUKHARA

mud-splattered lanes
radiating from the Centrum
delineate the Jewish quarter
of the distant, fabled Bukhara

from the Babylonian Exile
this hardy, ancient tribe
moved northward to the Kara Kum
while others turned
    to Canaan in the south

a figure stands on Tsentralnaya
clutching a ruddy, swaddled babe
    to her brightly-covered bosom -
    beyond, an iron-gated court
    encompassing the synagogue

we smile, the universal crutch,
when there is no other sign
    nor language to pursue
I try to feel the unsaid warmth,
    the patriarchal pedigree
from father Abraham to this day -
    but, as with the Yemenite, -
    the Falasha, or Cochin,
      we are galaxies apart

      until . . .
with gentleness she hands me
    the infant from her arms

and then . . .
I hear the lilting melodies
from the modest House of God,
as faintly,
the strains of Hebrew prayer
waft through the chilly Sabbath air

this, then, is it! . . .
the chain of commonality
forged by five millennia

delivering the child to mother,
I turn to enter the courtyard,
offering *"Shabbat Shalom"*

"Shabbat Shalom,"
she echoes back,
"Shabbat Shalom!"

Mission to Uzbekistan - "Dudel" is David Carabet, age 93, who now resides in California. His son, Dr. Norman Carabet, Arlene Levand, Judith Tower and the author, formed the search team that found Ruvain Carabet in Tashkent.

MISSION TO UZBEKISTAN
(Ruvain's Odyssey

Czernowitz, 1919 - civil upheaval abounds -
a difficult time for Ruvain to bid goodbye
to his friend and uncle, Dudel, not much older,
    but off to America . . .

ahead, for those who chose to stay behind,
decades of famine and bloodiest of wars,
Stalinist promises never fulfilled -

"es ist shwer zu zein a Yid!"

when the nazis invade Mother Russia's land,
he charges onward and eastward, an odyssey
across the flat steppes and over the Urals
one step ahead of the thundering Hun

       * * * *

armed with an address from twenty years back,
Dudel's son embarks on a search-and-find mission,
on this Sunday afternoon, in October '85,
to find Ruvain in Tashkent, very much alive -

after fruitless hours of growing frustration
we enter the apartment complex, at last -
announcing ourselves, he adamantly refuses
to even open the door for us

living a lifetime in fear has taken its toll,
but at his wife's insistence he soon relents -
quickly immersed in a whirlpool of emotions,
greetings and reminiscences take over the scene -

"Dudeleh, I hope you are well! I am with
your son, Dudeleh! It has been so many
years . . . Be well, Dudeleh . . . Be well!"

Ruvain smiles into the video-camera,
waving to the unseen . . .reunion complete

"es ist shwer zu zein a Yid!"

GROSSMAN, THE DUPE ?

Stately Leningrad has had its tragic time,
"The Siege" memorialized in every public place -
now that more than forty years have passed,
this volatile "Petrograd" lives on in glory

Gregory Grossman stands erect and proud
in the once-elegant synagogue hall

"I am Grigor, President of this
congregation . . ."

and from that point on he drones
in obvious apologist tones,
offering every conceivable excuse
for the State's chosen right to refuse

my regurgitating mind harkens back
  to the Judenrat of Lodz and Vilna,
performing ugly tasks that, if not done,
would be carried out by bestial brutes

caught in this maelstrom of dilemma,
the councils rarely had a better choice,
eventually joining their brethren in death

my last question answered, like the others,
              innocuously,
Grigor graciously bids goodbye, and pitches:

"Tell everyone in U-S-A to visit
my lovely shul!"

I turn away and snicker, facetiously,
(aside)

"Sure, sure, comrade - now hurry off
to the KGB, and give your daily report!"

then I thought

someone had to head those councils
someone has to be President here

why not Grossman?
why not, indeed!

Yevtushenko is the most gifted and famous Russian poet. Thousands crowd halls and public squares to hear him read his works. The search for truth is the underlying theme of much of his poetry. *"Babi Yar"* (1961) was written as a poignant outcry against the centuries-old anti-Judaism so vicious in the Russia of yesterday and today. It was hailed as well as assailed by critics. This was his first and last attempt to speak out on the sensitive issue.

LETTER TO YEVTUSHENKO

Yevtushenko - I am here!
For the past month I have seen
your "Matushka Rossiya"
from north to south,
from east to west
from the canals and palaces
of Leningrad,
your "Venice of the north,"
to the magnificent
mosques of Samarkand -
from the majesty of Red Square,
to Tashkent's remote cosmopolis -
from Novgorod's ancient kremlin,
to the onion-domes of Suzdal -
from Vladimir's provincial charm,
to Bukhara's silk-route culture -
the vastness and the differences,
the beauty and the mystery,
have notably impressed me -
I salute your grand and glorious homeland

Yevgeny Alexsandrovitch Yevtushenko -
please follow me clearly -
when you wrote of Babi Yar
so many years ago,
you saw yourself as a Jew,
a *"Zhid"* in your native tongue

"Over Babi Yar
there are no memorials.
The steep hillside like a rough
                 inscription.
I am frightened.
Today I am as old as the Jewish race.
I seem to myself a Jew at this moment.
1, wandering in Egypt.
I, crucified. I, perishing . . . ."

a clever ruse, my comrade!
but your petty protestations,
eloquent though they were,
fell upon deaf ears . . .
then, and now, deaf ears -
do you understand? -deaf, mute!
your feeble attempt to appeal
to a bigot-infested system
of perverted anti-Zhid mentality
was a noble effort, Yevgeny,
but it failed miserably

"I am also a boy in Bialystok,
    the dropping blood spreads across
            the   floor,
    the public-bar heroes are rioting
    in an equal stench of garlic and
            of drink . . .
    . . . the corn-chandler is beating-up
        my   mother."

the Einsatzgruppen trigger-pullers
in that pastoral-looking ravine
called Babi Yar, a name that will
remain uppermost in the annals
of history's most dastardly acts,
needed no excuse for what they did -
the madmen of the Reich and
their robotic, savage cadres
took full responsibility for
their "war against the Jews" -
they were, from the beginning,
completely honest and direct
about their aim for a Jew-less world -
you have read "Mein Kampf", of course -
it's all there!

the 'Final Solution' formula
adopted at Wansee, during a
most substantial cocktail lunch,
was merely the culmination of
an insidious thought-process
which soon became habitual,
eventually developing into
a firmly-implanted belief system -
an attitude, if you will -
and you must know, Yevtushenko,
nothing short of a frontal lobotomy
permanently changes a personality -

in this case, a team of surgeons,
Doctors Eisenhower, Patton,
Montgomery and your Zhukov,
eliminated the symptoms -
but not the bacillus -
        never the disease!

"And I am one silent cry
over the many thousands
        of the buried;
am every old man killed here,
every child killed here.
O my Russian people I know you . . .

How horrible is that pompous title
the anti-semites call themselves,
Society of the Russian Race."

as for you, dear "Zhenka,"
you are not being honest with us -
you play to your readership,
you are revered universally
you take stands on human rights -
but what has become of your
unpopular role as a *Zhid*?
why have you not carried on
with this intriguing thought?
your "Babi Yar" exposed the
wounds for all the world to see -

"When the last anti-semite on earth
        is buried forever
let the *Internationale* ring out
No Jewish blood runs among my
blood, but I am bitterly and heartily
hated
        as if I were a Jew.
By this, I am a Russian."

now you must continue with this theme -
"Zhenka," I implore you here and now -
go to your study, or sit under a birch -
walk the pathways near your dacha,
or recline along the river-bank,
and take up your honored pen -
write a new "Babi Yar" - a "Babi Yar"
        for the Mother Russia of today!

Regain the lofty position you deserve -
Step forward, "Zhenka"!

                more power to the poets!

                with undying hope for peace,
                and love, and brotherhood, I am,
                Stuart Farrell Tower

Epilogue

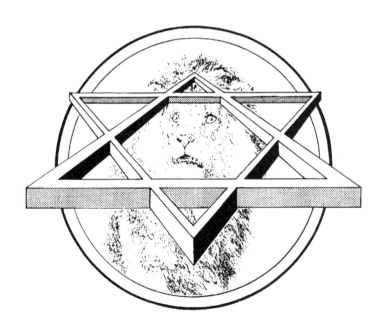

I.

2050

Enter:

Four Horsemen of the Judaic Apocalypse

Apathy

Amorality

Apostasy

Assimilation

in the wake of a pending painless tribulation
as we move blithely into the century ahead,
who will step forth and speak for the dead

of

a

silent

holocaust?

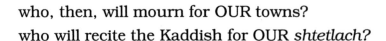

who, then, will mourn for OUR towns?
who will recite the Kaddish for OUR *shtetlach?*

    for Skokie and Morton Grove?
    for Westchester County, Great Neck or
        Crown Heights?
    for Brookline, Newton or Randolph?
    for Bloomfield Hills or Shaker Heights,
        or
    Bethesda, East Orange or St. Louis Park?
    for Florida's vast "pale of settlement" ?

who will grieve for the City of Angels?
who will beat their breast for Westwood?
who will bear witness for Woodland Hills?

who will even care to ask

    "where
      are
        your
          Jews
            today"?

II.

VOICES

Shema Yisroel!
Hearken to these words . . .
Weep and wail no more!

Ye, whose tears have
salted a thousand rivers
from the Jordan to the Danube,
from the Volga to the Rhine . . .
Ye must weep no more!

Ye, whose blood has drenched
a million bricks and stones,
from the Temple's western wall
to the pinnacles of pyramids,
from the ramparts of the ghetto
to the holocaust halls of terror . . .
Shema Yisroel!
Ye children of God
        must no longer cry!

Nay, not one more drop,
not one more curdling wail,
even for those who suffer still
under the yoke of tyranny . . .
                    for
tears do not bring sunlight,
                    nor freedom,
nor peace for Yisroel . . .
                    and
your cries would only fall
upon indifferent ears!

Shema   Yisroel!
Hear this well,
O Children of Destiny . . .
          Sanctify and Amplify
the sounds of yesterday,
          Magnify your legacy of
                    Voices!

Beginning as a whisper
from far beyond the storm,
gathering in growing strength,
emerging from the Gulags of time . . .

the stifled moans of those
who perished on the racks of
       Inquisition,
the haunting cries of Babi Yar,
as they scream *"vergess uns nisht!"*

It is the voice of Akibah
in the courtyard of his death,
a vow of faith with his final breath,
       and
the *"desaparecidos,"* disappeared ones
of the Argentine,
with fading shouts of
"Recuerdenos . . . Remember us!"

Hear the chant of the Falasha
      remnant,
as they roam Ethiopian hills
with a hopeful "Bring us home . . .
o bring us home!"

Listen to Jonathan, Proud Eagle
      of Entebbe,
counting cadence for the Lord's
      Brigade
for the looming Battle of Redemption

      Yes!
Sanctify and Amplify
these sounds of yesterday...
Magnify your legacy of Voices!

Now,
blast the ram's horn
loud and clear,
for all the world
to heed and hear,
echoing through
the Land of Zion,
like the bellowing roar
of the mighty lion!

Shema Yisroel ! - Hear 0 Israel!
We shall never be silent again

". . . and thou shalt teach these words
diligently unto thy children,
and they to their children . . .
and unto their children's children . . .
forevermore!"

Shema Yisroel! - Hear 0 Israel!

TOMORROWS HOPE

with you, my dearest ones, I share these thoughts,
and leave to you the keys to a treasure chest
    of wisdom, understanding and compassion,
    the legacy to which you were born,
    the law of God as written in the Book

throughout the generations, for millennia to come,
it is the young, the youthful
    who can stand erect,
it is the young
    who step forth to meet the challenge
it is the young
    who demonstrate a thirst for knowledge,
it is the young
    who rapidly absorb the Words

therefore, it is for you to delve into these truths
and diligently pass them on unto **your** children

now, rally around this glowing torch of heritage,
the eternal light that brightly shows the way,
grasp it firmly in your hands,
                and carry on!

    With a grandfather's love
    and ever-present hope.

to the *aineklach:*
Shane Eli Tower Cohn
Dariel Lee Cohn
Eric Michael Bloom
Cayla Ann Bloom

ACKNOWLEDGMENTS

A very special, love-wrapped gratitude to my fair lady, Roslyn, for her sounding-board encouragement and the ever-ready helping hand she so graciously gives. Her expert driving, complemented by my near-error-free navigating, delivered us safely, and sometimes calmly, through the pot-holed lanes of rural Eastern Europe and the cobbled mazes of its urban jungles, during our most recent journeys of old world discovery.

Sincerest thanks to the following most gracious people for sharing their time and thoughts during my Eastern European and USSR travels, 1980-1993. We managed to muddle through the various language barriers with a cacophonous combination of attempted Polish, Hungarian, Romanian, Bulgarian, Russian, Uzbek, Yugoslavian, Czech and the more common bonds of English, Yiddish and "Yinglish" - each frustratingly punctuated by the inevitable gesturing and finger-pointing:

POLAND: Gavriel ?, Warsaw; Reb Mendele Lebovicz, Crakow
Rabbi Michael Shudrich, Warsaw

CZECH REPUBLIC/SLOVAKIA: Moshe Haver, Prague;
Veronica Zhouf, Prague

HUNGARY: Gyula* and Suri Drechsler, Budapest; Jakob Glaser, Budapest; Robert Ben Turin, Budapest

The former **YUGOSLAVIA:** Lazar Obican, Dubrovnik; Emilio Tolentino, Dubrovnik; Rivka Pardo Shlossberg, Sarajevo

BULGARIA: Anatole Naftashin, Sofia

ROMANIA: Eduard Adler, Brasov; Reb Shimon Fleisher, Bucharest
Iancu Livadaru, Bucharest; Yossi Nachman, Brasov; Daniel Regenstreif, Bucharest; Chief Rabbi, Moshe Rosen*, Bucharest

The former **SOVIET UNION:** Ruvain Carabet*, Tashkent, Uzbekistan
Grigor Grossman, Leningrad (St. Petersburg); Mira Kohan, Samarkand, Uzbekistan; Hershel, Ilena and Artur Maidel, Tashkent; Eliahu Ben Moshe, Bukhara, Uzbekistan; Menachem Efraim Ben Moshe, Samarkand

David and Mila Shrayer, Moscow (now of Providence, R.I.)

FINLAND: Sholom Bolotofsky, Helsinki

* known to be deceased

BY THE AUTHOR

"Hear 0 Israel" - poetica Judaica
(Paideia House, NY, Los Angeles, London, 1983)

"Treblinka" (from "The Stone Forest Trilogy")
(Editor's Choice Award, National Library of Poetry, 1994)

"Kaddish for Our Times"
(*Jewish Life,* Union of Orthodox Jewish Congregations, 1974*)*

"The Hand That Held The Dagger"
(*Voices, Israel 1980* - an anthology of diaspora writers and poets)

"Cults, Missionaries and Jewish Youth"
(lecture circuit, 1976-1983)

"Boone, Israel and the Jews"
(feature article, Anglo-Jewish press, throughout North America)

"The Missionary Menace"
(feature article, Anglo-Jewish press, throughout North America)

"The Calvert (Texas) Jewish Cemetery"
(feature article, *Texas Jewish Post and Opinion*)

"Where Have You Gone, Bob Dylan?"
(lecture series-The Christian missionary movement-its outreach to Jewish youth)

SUGGESTED READING:

One of the most comprehensive, well-defined bibliographies on the subject of Eastern European Jewry just before and during the Shoah, can be found in Martin Berenbaum's **The World Must Know - The History of the Holocaust as told in The United States Holocaust Memorial Museum** (Little Brown and Company, Boston, New York, 1993, bibliographical notes, pages 224-232). Additionally, the fine works of Martin Gilbert, Lucy Davidowicz, Gerald Reitlinger and other recognized students of the era contain exhaustive references.

While this clearly shows an avalanche of material on the subject, precious little has been written about the aftermath and those survivors who chose to remain in Eastern Europe. I cite the following for your interest:

A non-Jewish Polish photo-essayist, Malgorzata Niezabitowska, along with Tomacz Tomaczewski, has published a poignant and handsome book, **Remnants: The Last Jews of Poland** (Friendly Press, NY, 1986).

Yale Strom, a renowned musicologist and documentarian, has travelled extensively throughout Eastern Europe, and has filmed an excellent documentary **The Last Jews of Radauti** (Romania), and has published **A Tree Still Stands- Jewish Youth in Eastern Europe Today,** a photo-documentary (Philomel Books, Putnam Publishing, NY: 1990).

Ruth Ellen Gruber's **Jewish Heritage Travel - a Guide through Central and Eastern Europe** (John Wiley and Sons, NY, 1992) is exceptionally informative for those planning investigative touring. I am indebted to her as well as Bernard Postal and Samuel Abramson for their definitive **Travelers Guide to Jewish Landmarks of Europe** (Fleet Press, NY, 1971 -revised in 1980). Both have been invaluable in helping me plan my travels in the region during the past twelve years.

Withered Roots is offered as a singular tribute to those who stayed on, worked hard to eat and live, raised families, endured the many hardships of the post-war communist era, and are continuing to survive and even thrive in the midst of confusion and chaos that mark today's new poltics in Eastern Europe.

Stuart F. Tower

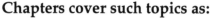
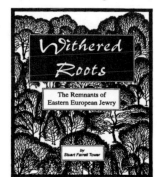